AF522641

The Ignoble Strife

THE IGNOBLE STRIFE

Dr. Balbir Singh

OMEGA PUBLICATIONS
NEW DELHI 110002 (INDIA)

OMEGA PUBLICATIONS
4378/4B, G4, JMD House, Murari Lal Street,
Ansari Road, Daryaganj, New Delhi-110 002
Phone: 23278062, 65901906
e-mail: omega_publications@yahoo.com

Head Office :
79/23, Laxmi Garden,
Near Satya Jyoti School,
Gurgaon (Haryana)

First Published, 2011

ISBN-978-81-8455-283-6

PRINTED IN INDIA

Printed at Tarun Offset Printers, Delhi - 110053

For my dear sons

RANDEEP AND KARANDEEP

The time is out of joint, O cursed spite,
  That ever I was born to set it right!

—William Shakespeare, *Hamlet*

Time to Die Alone and Other Poems
The Early Fiction of Philip Roth
The Chaotic Age
Badalte Mausham (Hindi)

Foreword

Though Balbir Singh has been known to me for a long time, I felt a pleasant surprise when one morning he came to present me a copy of his first book of poems. After that I received his other books also. I admit that his poems have left an indelible impression on me. This is perhaps because I am acutely aware of the necessity of morality in public life and Balbir Singh in his poetry rakes up moral issues with a rare intensity.

I have been in public life for many years and so find little time to indulge in poetry. But we used to read the poems of such Romantic poets as Wordsworth, Keats, Byron, etc. besides modern realistic poetry when we were students in Punjab University, Chandigarh. Singh's poetry is romantic inasmuch as he portrays the emotions of nostalgia, desires, aspirations, failures and frustrations of man. But in my opinion he is more a realist as he portrays loss of moral values and decay in modern society. In fact, his artistic achievement lies more in expressing universal human predicament than in any limited or narrow vision—social, philosophical or political. I hope the poems in the present anthology will go a long way in making the reader conscious of the ills in contemporary social system and of the inevitability of their manifestation in the individual's response to his environment. I wish him success in his avocation.

Ved Pal

Formerly,
Deputy Speaker,
Haryana Vidhan Sabha,
and

Chairman,
Haryana State Agricultural Marketing Board

25-9-2010
Karnal

Preface

Past joys do not haunt man. But past pain does. Even the slightest, the smallest. And when it haunts him beyond a tolerable point, he compulsively expresses it, gives it shape either in words, colours, sculpure or rhythmic notes. But all people don't or can't do it. Only those with special sensibility and capability for handling different tools (words, in case of poetry) do it. The sharper the pain, the more severe the intensity of the emotions expressed and consequently more the joy derived out of it by the poet and the reader alike. All people don't relish reading poetry. Only a few of them are capable of this joy, as only the mighty enjoy wrestling bouts with total understanding.

Newton Arvin remarked that now we put a premium on a poetry which seems difficult, which is "emotionally perplexed, intellectually hard-earned, stylistically dense" with the result that we fail to do justice to "poets who 'signified' no more, or not much more, than they plainly stated." So it is possible that to some my poetry may be of not much worth. But in my opinion the first principle of poetry is that it should provide joy of a higher kind. Poetry is neither total joy nor total moralizing. It is both, mutually inclusive. I agree with Coleridge, who once observed, "If poetry instructs, it does so only through pleasure". I write for the common people who have a taste for poetry. In these poems also my endeavor has been to present my vision through simple images in an easy style so that all can enjoy them.

Karnal

Dr. Balbir Singh

Contents

1. The Variety of Humanity

All are not so lucky, here,
power is not for everyone,
wisdom is denied to many.
All are not blessed with
super genius or mighty
physique or the Greek beauty.

A great majority of them
are physical wrecks,
social failures, domestic fiasco,
misfit in the working place,
hopeless sons, deplorable fathers,
poor husbands, despised neighbors.

All are not equal or same.
The world is not a garden,
carefully maintained and preserved.
This is, at best, the natural jungle,
some spots here and there
ravishingly beautiful.

Some common scenery of hills,
some dull patches here,
and stinking mounds
of garbage in some corners.
This is the variety
of the life of the humans.

2. The Terrible Phase of History

The time has perhaps come
to go back in the past;
a daunting, gloomy journey
against the current of time,
like a motor moving backward
through the crowd
of traffic fast moving forward.

To live like those solitary
beasts in the jungle, living alone.
Weak and timid,
brave and mighty,
alike; because life simply
has to be faced alone.
As death.

Either the civilization
has reached the last point,
has come full circle;
or this is a phase of history.
A very cruel phase;
like that of the notorious tyrants,
brandishing their cutlass.

Hopefully it will also pass.
Like theirs.

3. Human Brotherhood

Is it worth it?
The sweat and the strivings,
for the community of humans.
For one's great country,
noble birth in a reputed tribe,
city, locality, the relatives
and the members of family.
All kinds of sacrifices.

They don't mitigate your pain.
An ulcer, an injury and illness
has to be borne alone,
and, above all, death.
You don't share your wealth
or property with them.
Nobody likes to part with
a single dime for others.

Then why do they matter so?
All the wars fought for them
and even with them.
A man lives, and sometimes dies
solely for them,
and so cannot ignore them.

Society gives so miserly.
Gives meanly but demands liberally.

4. Envy

Hatred and vengeance
have some base and logic
and justified foundation.
But this green eyed monster
hits you without rhyme or reason.

Carnal passion for
the creature of opposite sex
can be explained and justified;
to procreate your kind,
though it is fetish nowadays.

But jealousy has no purpose;
because so many people
can live on this earth peacefully.
There is enough for all.

It infects even children;
youths are often its victims.
But it gobbles up the elderly
so greedily and totally.

They are most vulnerable
to its poisonous attack.
They sometime bite their
own bodies in fury
like the venomous snake.

It wants to destroy its object.
But it is two pronged cutlass.
It also burns its own host,
who rears it, nourishes it.

It slowly gnaws at the inner vitals
of the human being
who has born it and cherished it,
and makes him hollow from within.

Its object may be eliminated
or may survive.
But its fire is not extinguished
and burns peace to ashes.

The envious man
is surely doomed for ever.
And happiness eludes him
like a mirage in desert.

* * *

5. Raw Society

In this raw society
only raw things count;
raw alcohol, raw sex, raw relations.
Refinement is a thing of the past.
Raw items like money matter.

The guards are guarding
only the guardians.
The real beacons holding
the torch of sane humanity
are exposed to raw bullets.

Even the wives refuse
to understand them,
the children and the taught,
let alone the sea of the unknown
and the unknowing humanity.

They also judge your worth
who are themselves worthless,
(sometimes they are the only judges)
who barter happiness for money
and try to buy peace.

* * *

6. Taking on Evil

Evil must be faced sternly;
resisted and tackled,
by gripping it tightly by the horns
and pushing it back
with full will and force.

Simply because it cannot be
eradicated ones and for all.
It will sprout again and again
through millions of pores
in this life giving earth.

So the fight must go on forever.
Otherwise in no time
it will cover the world like
unchecked weeds and
make its virgin beauty stink.

You can see the evidence
in history of humanity
since the fierce struggle
between Suras and Asuras,
to the modern Hitlers and Ladens.

Its presence cannot be ruled out
ignored or connived at.
We must be always ready
to take on the enemy
and vanquish it.

* * *

7. The Prisoners

Men or women--all are prisoners.
Child, youth, or old,
rich or poor, weak or strong.
No one can ever be free
from that first anguished cry
to the last whimper of death.

No one can cross
the barriers of time, space,
age, money and power,
personal, social or physical.

In the bigger cell
sometimes the prisoner
has the feeling that he is free.
That is all, we are allowed
to beguile our time
in apparent joy and peace.

Even we can't rise up
too much from the earth.
It pulls us down mercilessly.
Enjoy the freedom of the prison!

* * *

8. The Annals of Humans

What was that I lived for
two score years; inscribed:
from Nineteen Fifty to Ninety?
Life span in a book of history,
some pages, half page
or only a few lines
in the annals of humans.

Still so, in the known history.
In unwritten and unknown
innumerable people lived
their life and died.
On a river bank, in a jungle,
life in a hut on a sea shore,
in palaces amidst luxuries.

To secure a little corner,
the same designs,
all full of same desires,
passions and obsessions;
to expand the territory,
to win the worlds,
or to win the self and soul.

If all trod the same path
if all felt tired and gave up
the frantic pursuance
and just relaxed!
What would have been
the fate of human history
and the future course?

* * *

9. Solutions

My father couldn't find solution
though he thought and thought
a lot of thoughts,
searched and researched;
with that old-fashioned cup
in hand, or a cigarette
dangling in his old fingers;
serious and thoughtful.

Nor could I find,
though I tried my best
in my humble way.
Sometimes in his style also.
I doubt my son
will be able to make it,
and untie the knot
of the secrets of life.

It takes years and generations
to achieve something,
to invent some new idea or device.
The smallest contribution
to the collections of humanity.
Trophies of culture have not come
by pushing a button,
in an instant, easily.

Or by amassing mounds of wealth
in dollars or pounds,
or by wielding the wand
of authority and power.
Dynasties advance from
old generations to the new.
Civilization does not progress
in conventional thrusts.

It takes years
of perspiration and inspiration,
frenzy of madness for a target,
or the greatest sacrifice,
some noble original thought
worth laying down one's life,
to add something worthwhile
to the already accumulated.

* * *

10. The Overlapping Generations

Poised momentarily on
the dividing wall of life,
I glance over the two sides
and wonder, after all,
which one is better, preferable
(though there is no choice at all).

On which I am stepping on,
(in fact, already with them)
or the one I have trampled on.
Because in my youth,
the elders seemed formidable,
like mighty giants.

They dictated to us, younger,
how to go about life
and controlled everything—
means to livelihood, dignity,
enjoyments, power and money,
the course of our life.

And now it seems
youths don't look to us, for help.
They have sway over everything.
They are focal point of all,
the society, the parties,
the gathering of humans.

Everything revolves around them,
parents, friends and girls.
Everything is for them,
gadgets, discourse and fun,
war, chivalry and honour
and what man fights for.

The whole drama and the show
rushing into their whirlpool.
The pivot, the crown of creation.
All the inventions, fashions,
the progress of civilization
is by them, about them, for them.

All others serve and adore them
till they reach the fateful boundary.
I feel dumped with the lesser mortals,
with the lack-lustres, surplus,
bringing in limelight the hero,
like the team of extras.

It has always been so.
Because I am no more one of them.
Or perhaps times have changed,
priorities have shifted,
as they always do
with ever new generations.

* * *

11. Unity in Diversity

Sipping my coffee at the café
at Rashtrapati Nivas at Shimla
I wondered at the variety
of visitors from far and near.

Fair from north, dark from south,
short, tall, rich and poor,
speaking all sorts of tongues;
Oriya, Kannad, Punjabi and others.

Even some of British origin,
whose forefathers built
the mansion in the last part
of golden nineteenth century.

What kind of country ours is,
I wondered.
These people welcomed all—
the Rippons and the Macaulays,
the Marco Polos, the Huns,
the Pathans, and the Moghuls.

All were welcomed.
This is the real thing.

And they dwelled here;
became a part of this country,
imbibed its spirit by and by
and turned Hindustani.

Of all religions and colours,
of all creeds and castes.
I was sure no other country
has so much variety.
This is a miracle they remained
unified for so many years.

* * *

12. Old Things

How soon the things
become old and redundant.
My typewriter is lying in a corner,
dusty and dead.

(How excited I was
when I bought it some time ago.)
It's replaced by the sleek processor,
working so smoothly, easily.

Old cars, old phones, old houses!
So are the people.
And the people's dreams,
failed, licking the dust.

The famous dandy of yore
turned grey-haired,
wrinkled and ugly middle-aged;
frightened at his own image.

The old guards in the village,
assertive and commanding;
respected, feared and obeyed,
forgot the long stride of time.

Now sitting under the tree, alone

they are friendless and forlorn,
without even a silent listener,
deserted by their former hangers-on.

Dreams grow old faster, and die.
You realize very soon
that they have not been fulfilled,
simply cannot be fulfilled.

In a vast and turbulent sea
the silly dreams of a small fish
do not matter in the least,
grand though they may seem.

She may move here and there,
cry in pain or pray,
but she can't change things
nor can retard the decay.

* * *

13. All Escapes Are Temporary

I only demanded
escape for a few moments,
(tired by the weary round
of day's drudgery)
foray into the alleys of romance.
But it was blatantly refused.

And they said, "Stay at home.
Don't run away".
What can a man do or say?
Yoked to domestic duties, ever,
social commitments,
bondages, shackles, heavy harness.
Life is only this,
in this crowd of humans.

Simple orgies are often
overshadowed by bleak preaching.
Not much to heart's talk,
still less to listen to some melody.
There is a flat 'No' to every wish.
Where to live? And how to live?

I had begun the evening
really jolly, joyous,
but hardly had taken off

the concrete ground when
the voices confronted me,
pouring down like unabated
torrents of rain, through
the door, windows, all sides.

Menacing gestures were made,
wild signs of premonitions,
flinging arms, foreboding nods,
in the name of austerity,
social, domestic responsibilities,
harsh official explanation,
ruined reputation and neglected duty,
our rich culture, in particular.

In short, the evening was spoiled.
A small person's small happiness.
I am not for avoiding my duty.
I know all escapes are temporary.
And so they don't provide
permanent solutions and solace.

But to be glued ever
to the dreadful reality,
like the legendary ox to the oil mill,
moving round, round and round,
is not acceptable to all.
One has a right to escape
sometimes, though one must return
soon, safe and sane.

* * *

14. No One Cares

Who knows and who cares,
what is right and what is wrong,
for whom good, for whom bad?

A bear picks up a living fish
casually and easily
from shallow water and eats it.

The flesh of a living fish,
red hot spicy organs of a writhing
and, perhaps, crying creature.

One can imagine
the horror, anger and pain,
when the reveler relishes its prey.

Then throws away bones and remains
and licks its blood-stained paws.
No one bothers or sympathizes.

* * *

15. Out of Control

There was a time
when everything seemed
compact, and in total control;
health, finance, desires.

Single man and his sole pursuits.
Now all things seem
to be out of control,
flying outwardly with centrifugal force.

Physique, blood pressure, diabetes;
children, wife, relationships;
family, country, society;
riots, crimes, hazards.

Nothing seems to be safe,
secure, chaste and intact.
Is it due to my own age
or the history has reached this stage?

Rolling time changes things,
perhaps the era has crossed
that golden threshold
from where only decline starts.

* * *

16. Till Death Separates Us

Scarcely had I finished my meal
when my wife announced:
"Mrs. Mida is dead,
they just returned from the doctor".

Just a hundred yards away;
I left the table hurriedly
and walked to her house.
An eerie silence
(only Mr. Mida and a servant
took her to the doctor).

Her body lying on the floor;
pale, motionless, dead Mrs. Mida.
Mr. Mida lay limply on the bed,
shocked, unprepared for death;
people were slowly pouring in,
and tried to console him.

He was explaining the death,
in a dazed, defending voice.
Then began groaning,
and making feverish phone calls.

Male relatives, solemn, consoling;
female relatives mourning.

breast beating, crying, uttering
confused and choked phrases.

I wondered how he was feeling
about her demise;
sad, that she left him alone
(all children now married).

Perhaps feeling relieved also.
I recalled all the quarrelling,
shouting and nagging,
bitterness, hatred and suffering.
How she swore at him
when in the state of living!

Now he could gamble freely,
drink as much as he liked,
visit his beloved openly.
But he must have been
sorry for his children,
who had become motherless.

One does not feel attached
to the partner as to the children.
He must have felt more grief
over his mother's demise
than when the mother
of his children died.

* * *

17. Pity

I took my old, decrepit uncle
to the hospital, looked after him,
kept a vigil at his bedside
for three nights till he recovered.

Diseases in old age!
No parents, no wife, no sons.
Writhing in pain alone he was
on the verge; moreover, penniless.

My heart melts without any logic;
I was driven just by mercy
to serve the old man,
without any hidden motive.

And during all this time
I was in constant tension,
haunted by my boss;
petty agent of petty woes.

Bent upon humiliating me,
burning with jealousy inborn
boundless ego, futile rivalry
and desire to enjoy alone.

The skinny black hound!
Only because I was better than
he, and was liked and praised.
Man is the worst enemy of man.

So these humans behave.
Mean, envious, greedy,
sadistic, revengeful, and bully,
when unbridled power they have.

Like their ancestors, they are
mischievous, cruel, merciless;
but poor, wretched and pitiable
when in pain, they are helpless.

Still, buried deep, flows the fountain.
I know after some years
if I find my boss helpless, so,
I will feel pity on him also.

* * *

18. Privacy

There is no privacy here.
All your money, letters, papers are
exposed to the prying eyes of others;
and sanctity of living violated.

You can't claim a cabin
only for yourself.
If you have, you can't lock it,
not even a small cupboard.

Not even love making is feasible
freely in a room of your own,
and in such a small family,
even if the children are not around.

I remember my grandfather
living in the common living place
of the whole tribe.
He enjoyed his nights and days
with brothers, cousins, uncles,
(and children when they chose).

He just came to home
for eating his food twice a day,
(I wonder he ever loved his old woman),
otherwise talked, sat and shaved

in that big common drawing room
with bamboo cots lying around.

In the open, at the well ramp
he washed his clothes and himself
and went to fields for nature's call.
He did not know private life,
for him it was only among people,
walking, talking, working with them.

I wonder how it feels
without peers and neighbours,
living in a lonely house
in solitary hills bereft of humans.

The whole group around him
intruded in his privacy,
but all of them surrounded his
bed, when he fell sick, to die.

The whole town wishes you well,
and at your disposal in crisis,
willingly or unwillingly;
though when lately you were drunk
it was the talk of the town.
That is what the old society was.

Now I don't know
the man next door,
nor does he greet me.
He is least bothered
when I face human crisis.
I never pry into his affairs.

And still I prefer to live
in an apartment building
in a sea of faces, known, unknown,
but of my own kind.

On the one hand
there is the dread of the unknown,
and on the other, the fear
of encroachment by the known.

* * *

19. Her Survival

She survived hopefully,
with all her puppies safe
in a cozy corner of the street,
crouched securely at her breast.

She meekly bowed to her superiors.
Always greeted my pet,
her stronger neighbour
by wagging her tail, licking her.

And paid her obeisance,
all fours in the air,
accepting the other's power,
with humility and grace.

More over, expressing it loudly.
She never confronted the big bully
nor fought any useless brawl.
And ensured her survival.

* * *

20. Searching for a Pattern

Tom died today while holidaying on a remote beach
with all his pains, dreams and secret desires.
John's wife eloped with his fast friend,
she could not be traced yet, alive or dead.

A woman killed her husband, her children,
and is now in jail, repenting or enjoying, who knows?
A man of repute was thrashed in common street
among the crowd of common people.

Hard working farmers suffering the drought,
corrupt, cruel officials fleecing the honest,
politicians manipulating the affairs, and the people.
His son is married, her daughter is divorced.

And I am searching for the order, social or moral.
What should be done, ought not to be done.
In quest of a pattern in the loose disorder,
lawful obligations in the stark wilderness.

Look at the known history of the humans.
This has been, this is, and this will be thus.
The long annals of absurd anarchy and chaos.
What is the system, where is it, and who framed it?

* * *

21. Love

What is it, after all?
This attraction and infatuation,
this desire to see, meet, touch,
caress and embrace;
talk, help, support—all,
and then do fantastic things.
Everything about her
looks marvelous, sweet, fragrant.

Moon appears in her face
and roses in those cheeks.
What prompts such antics
which look awkward years after?
Something originates
in the recesses of the psyche
that feels the arrival of a person,
who wants other, is for other.

That is because of the urge
to create his replica.
Two instincts coalesce instantly,
recognition and assertion of self,
and procreation of one's own kind;
to make eternal this existence
through one's images
even after this body returns to dust.

Otherwise why a common person
so inflames the fancy,
so tightens the nerves
that the man is obsessed
with the two-legged creature
of opposite features.
Thus His sacred will is done
through strange ways.

* * *

22. Fighting

The little puppies fought
with each other, as if in earnest,
barking in infantile growl;
and the poor beasts
hardly able tó walk steadily.

The other day I saw
two school children
abusing each other in anger;
culminating in actual assault,
hate, anger, bruise and blood.

It comes so naturally, inborn.
Just like eating, sleeping, breeding.
And the youth,
rough, refined and uncouth
always shed blood, everywhere.

Grown ups and civilized,
mercifully, do it rather
non-violently, slyly, insidiously.
Big conspiracies for small things.
Street brawls among the poor and rich.

Why wonder, then, the battles
fierce and prolonged,

with the same beastly fury fought
in the long annals
of the whole mankind.

Though Darwin suggested
it was the struggle to exist
and only the fittest would survive.
But the Hitlers and the Tamburlaines
did it for something else.

The Akbars and the Ashokas,
the Edwards and the Tudors
could have avoided it.
The urge to fight is as intense
as to live in total peace.

No phase of human history passed
smoothly in peace, save some years.
And no period of war witnessed
ceaseless eternal encounters
without the peace that follows it.

* * *

23. Lilliputians

Are the stakes really high
in this small world
of still smaller things?
That man striving hard
to be in his boss's good books,
who himself licks the boots
of his own boss in a small office,
in a small city.

Other to get a luxury car,
another to grab a bungalow.
Lifelong despondency
for the disdainful beauty,
bitterly strained human relations.
What for, status and dignity?
which have already been lost
in the tardy process.

That is exactly
what the human history has been;
tribal hatred and revenge,
blood-shed for a tiny kingdom,
the Ashokas and Alexanderas
for the greater empires.
Are these high stakes?
Not high enough to shed blood.

But then, what are lofty ideals?
To meditate in the ancient hills,
for years and decades,
to achieve peace and contentment,
deliverance and salvation?
Who knows the mightier powers
look at us Lilliputians amusedly
like some giants.

Whatever kind of drama it may be,
it ends too soon
(sometimes suddenly and abruptly)
to encompass any grandiose issues.
Not like a leisurely Victorian novel,
rather like a short story,
where the climax and denouement
are reached soon.

Without detailed portrayal,
delving deep, or lengthy digressions.
How one blows up his ego and life
out of all proportion!
No one in this world is so low
as to feel disgraced.
And none so mighty and great
as to feel crowned.

* * *

24. The Branch of White Roses

In the cool early morning
when my forehead was burning
with the last night's orgies
and the rising day's onslaught;
when I was stepping out of home,
the long untrimmed tender
branch laden with roses
touched my head and face
like a beauty nudging me,
inviting me to love and caress.
Soft, slender, swinging young,
full of flowers, buds and bulbs.

And whispered in my ears
that life is still to live,
come what may,
howsoever scorching the sun.

It is not merely
the dead weight of worries,
but an invitation to visit this fair
of fun and frolic, joys and beauties.

* * *

25. The Central Pillars

The old are hopefully exempted
from the drudgery and strain,
let loose like the overworked
ox in his old age,
to roam free and relax.
The reward of a life time.

The children are even pampered
and encouraged
in their mischief and nuisance.
The young are warned,
sometime rebuked for their uproar,
but somehow always pardoned.

The revelries become them.
When will they do it if not now?
It is only us, the middle-aged
who bear the brunt of it all.
We are supposed to solve and resolve
all their whims and problems.

Fulfil the demand of wife for fun,
even when unwilling and drained
by the cruel human forces.
The children's and the youth's
demand for money to buy joy,
the old's for keeping fit, to live.

The boss goads for more work,
the neighbour for relaxations,
a friend in crisis for some favour,
to reconcile and to pacify;
all turn to us, the central pillars.
The crowns of responsibility.

But we have made so by Him.
A strong neck to bear the heavy yoke,
immune to slight ailments,
to the buffets of the rivals and baiters.
We have wisdom and experience
to absorb the shocks of upheavals.

And what we get when
we slide down to the edge and
look expectantly to the new players?
Not so much always.
But still, we have to oblige
as our elders have done.

* * *

26. If I Knew

If I had known the value of money
earlier, I would have perhaps
behaved and acted differently.
I would have discarded the balls
in the days of games and joys,
and run after money, the crisp notes.

In youth, I wouldn't have chased
rosy cheeks and swelling bosoms,
squandered valuable time and energy
after buxom beauties
for a few hot kisses and embraces
and some grotesque antics.

Instead, I would have utilized them
for better profits, hunting for
some brilliant, tinkling treasure.
But that I did not do since
I was content with what I was
and happy with what I had.

Moreover, ignorant of coming things,
unaware that gold makes all things golden,
physical, mental, moral and social;
like Midas, it glitters whatever it touches.
In its company all wishes come true,
virtues consummated, and dreams fulfilled.

Though all the prophets tell us
riches fail to bring true happiness.
Why, then, in my middle years
it has become the most coveted thing;
better than sports of childhood,
and orgies and whims of youth.

Some may crave it for these.
But my purpose is something else.
I just want it to avoid poverty
the harbinger of sufferings and insults.
The pigmy penury makes of a man!
The mother of most evils.

But who will sacrifice those three score
years for the present decade,
abandon present for the dim future?
Why, I should have prayed and prayed,
and ponder over the thick scriptures
casting it aside as my old dumb-bells.

And aspire for something higher
like everlasting peace or divine grace
and preparation for the next birth.
May be this phase also passes
like childhood and youth
and I stop craving it near my death.

* * *

27. The Connecting Link

They normally move in herds,
enjoy in groups,
fight in tribes,
like most of the mammals,
and even insects.
As when ants move
just like soldiers in columns.

If Darwin was right
then it explains many things,
clears many metaphysical doubts,
burning debates and confusions.
Just once we admit
the great and inseparable link
with our ancestors.

One is never inspired in a family
after a drink or two,
but one is enthralled
when drinking in a club,
among the elite rich,
or the crowd of the commons
in a shabby street, just like pigs.

The layers and layers
of civilization and culture,

over the years and years,
have wrapped the raw skeleton
with gaudy dresses;
still the attire is significant.
Nakedness is disgusting.

* * *

28. A Happy Day

Riding my bicycle on the green
highway, I hummed a romantic tune
of my happy adolescent days;
having prepared my lecture on Frost,
embraced my mother good bye
back home to village,
kissed my wife on the lips.
(She otherwise doesn't allow
that in daytime.)

This was a happy day.
Sparrows were chirping around,
calves were lying relaxed,
(crows poking them in their ears).
I imagined my department head,
the evil one can do some evil.
But if he does anything today,
I will hit him in the face,
that's all, I decided.
This is the only solution of evil.
To hit it back more forcefully.

The day, (well, not the whole day)
the moments were calm and tranquil.
Like a lake of clear blue water,
no mud, no weed, no vile creatures.

Sometimes it so happens.
But not always.
All the days are not the same.

But what was the guarantee?
I might get some bad news,
get transfer orders to other college,
or such myriad calamities,
till I go to bed tonight.
But I was happy at the moment.

* * *

29. The Glass Wall

They sang and danced
happily and noisily,
little sparrows, celebrating
the first shower of the season.

One of them, perched on my
window, started knocking
at the pane with its beak,
thak…thak…thak…thak.

I was startled to see
the little eyes staring at me
and the intermittent knock
as if calling me, to join them,
leaving my work.

How could I?
being a man of the world,
having things to do.
It was unfair of the little Dryad
to invite me so.

But perhaps she was not calling me.
Just trying to cross the pane
and enter the room,
not comprehending the transparency
of the glass wall.

For her there was no bar
between her airy world
and the dense world of humans.
Just forgetting reality
in her vain illusion,
to enjoy the romance of life.

Again the same ignorant
thak...thak…thak…thak,
like the puppy who starts barking
when it is refused food,
insisting for its share childishly.
He does not know that
nothing in this world comes easy.

The world does not give anything,
without its price;
the price of living life.
Like the landlord of the inn,
it charges a heavy price
for the brief sojourn.
He will learn the hard way
to wait patiently for the crumbs.

We are ignorant of the reality
of the glass wall between
self's desire and fulfillment,
visible and the invisible,
known and the unknown,
and incur much loss and pain.

* * *

30. The Moon above the Hills

At dawn, the beautiful moon,
sparkling white, laughing in my face,
spreading her bright glory all around,
showering her virginal beauty
over the pine trees and hills lofty.

Over the sea of greenery
interspersed with proud deodars,
I gulped many an eyeful
of her majestic grandeur.
Who knows when my vision blurs!

She was fully aware that
her guide or rival of the day time
would soon arrive on the horizon,
with all his dazzling ferocity
in the opposite east.

Moon, so higher than us, below,
more beautiful than us, ugly.
But this is fated.
Moon is moon, we are we.
She in her heaven, we on our earth.

What is the use of brooding over
he is mighty, she is fair,
you are rich, I am poor!
Find peace and contentment
in the happiness and joy of others.

* * *

31. A Palace among the Huts

He wants to be like a palace
among the huts,
towering over and above
all the petty others.

Though he could rise high
in a desert or on an island,
he always wished to be
a part of others, yet above them.

Thus the love of the self
dispels pity for all others,
dries the humane fountains
and causes evil and chaos.

* * *

32. The Party Began

And the party began in earnest.
With loud, maddening noise or music,
everybody came in motion with a start,
shaking the body and its parts,
lively, excitedly and frantically,
shivering with youth and love.

Energy and dreams infinite,
flaying arms, flushed faces,
bulging bosoms, twisting white
maiden waists, raw round buttocks.
I sat silently with my friends,
some old, others neither-young-nor-old.

The fat dull girl doubling her figure,
another swaying her unripe breasts,
a dark skinny maiden
twisting and shaking her body,
emulating a heart-throb of our time,
lacking grace but with a rare energy.

All was so unlike our days,
when our dream girls danced.
They looked so gorgeous,
beautiful, ravishing and young,
And we used to watch the magic
spell-bound, in high romance.

In fact, they were the heroes
and heroines of the present.
Just as we have had ours.
The day was theirs,
ours had been left far behind.
That was the real difference.

* * *

33. Peace

Don't be afraid, it will pass off soon.
A little pain
and the episode will be over;
like the burning tissue
slashed off by the expert surgeon;
the anguish, pangs, excitement,
and the following gloom,
everything will disappear.

Life is worth it,
when the burdens are off.
What is the use at all
of longings, desires, wishes,
heart-piercing heart-burns?
Fast flowing current of tension
melting into silent warm tears
and choked, convulsing sobs.

Just an overpowering dark sleep,
void senseless sightless,
and the millions dreams
flashing in the eyes black out,
like the flame crushed
between the thumb and finger,
sharp burning and piercing pain,
but just for a moment.

Then slowly but matter-of-factly
the dark clouds descend
over the fret and turbulence.
The peace, cold dark peace;
the peace that follows understanding,
that precedes understanding,
or without understanding.
Only silent peace.

* * *

34. The People and I

The music was flowing
regularly and smoothly,
like the sparkling water
majestically in a big river.
And evoked memories golden
of yore, and desires romantic,
of living and enjoying.

But my heart didn't take a flight
as it was disturbed by pain,
undeserved and futile.
Some drab happening of the day,
some small folly by a small peer,
wounds inflicted by the unfeeling,
cruel and prowling hunters.

Why do they spoil another's joy?
They didn't offer me a drink
the day I was penniless.
They don't feea a starving beggar.
They are not happy in my happiness,
nor can they share the pains
of a patient writhing alone.

Then what right have they
to mar the happiness of one?

Is society for me
or am I for them?
Should I sacrifice my joy for them,
or should they leave a heart alone,
to live as he wants?

Who can say!
The world is like this
and I should have a thicker hide.
Or may be I made a mistake
howsoever small,
or they expected too much
from an ordinary man.

* * *

35. Moral Edifice

He was begotten among the Fords,
I was reared in a stinking slushy slum,
he boasted of a high and noble caste,
I was poised at the lowest social end,
he learned quickly, always got a gold medal,
I was the only FAIL in my elementary class.

Why was so?

I could not understand and accept this
nor could deduct an answer
from all my sources of knowledge.
Was it destined from my birth?
Or was I fated to survive thus
after making my entry to this stage?

No, no religion—I don't believe in rebirth.

Is somebody chuckling watching me
go through this ordeal of life?
Does anyone bother the myriads of life forms
accidentally cropped up on the earth
like mushrooms in rainy season,
some big, some small, ugly and beautiful?

Mystery hidden in mystery!

Then why did they build
such a huge moral edifice,
to be demolished intermittently
by the thundering new generation?
Did it give temporal joy to them
or they thought it to be permanent?

* * *

36. The Simplest Path

His idiotic face beamed
with a smile and
he was his natural self,
as happy, as satisfied,
as foolish, as ever.

Muse never smiled on him;
nor goddess *Laxmi* showered
her gold, nor Apollo bestowed
his beauty and strength.
Born without any special gift.

He was not blessed
with wealth and power,
yet he enjoyed life
and he did not lack anything.

Moreover, he did not feel
lacking in something.
Happy and contended to his heart,
he played the game of life,
with ease, smile and zest.

He never grumbled in gloom,
and had the rare art

of not craving more.
There are many paths to happiness.
He took the simplest one.

* * *

37. Ecstasy in the Hut

In the shabby wooden hut
among the lowest layer of vulgar herd
in the Hades of the human earth,
the uncivilized crumbs of cohabitants,
I gulped down the full cup
of the burning chilled liquor,
looked around for some moments
and rose smoothly to heavenly heights.

Transcended the dirty boundaries
to be in a brighter and cosier world.
Soon it evoked the best moments
of the best age, which had passed
and visions vast and unlimited
abolishing all the petty obstacles
as if by a magic wand,
turning to gold all base metals.

The realization of all the wayward wishes
and the choicest dreams,
when life is not merely
wading through a dense jungle.
But floating lightly in the vast,
glittering, beautiful space

or sailing smoothly and gaily
on the blue water of infinite sea.

Oh! would the vision were conjured up
in an elite club of the socialites,
surrounded by the gaudily dressed,
fragrant friends, male and female,
rare wine and delicacies to be savoured,
flushed, passionate, eager faces
amid the songs and dance
of the gentry and the nobility!

Or in the lush hilly surroundings
where haply I would have seen
young Dharmendra, like Adonis,
singing of the bliss of youth,
of love, of the valley and lake;
stumbling voluptuously with his coy beloved
through snow-clad white slopes,
presenting a weird look.

That would have been some fulfilment
of long cherished dreams.
Oh! the vastness of human dreams
and his smallness!
Never does the human vision fail.
Only the liver fails or the heart fails,
desires linger like the sparks in the amber
of the old and decrepit frame.

* * *

38. The Rich and the Poor

You imagine living
with dignity and honour.
No, not at all,
they are for the rich.

Thinking of love,
temporary and momentary.
Dreamy feelings don't go
with rough and hard penury.

They are the luxuries of the rich,
not the necessities of the poor,
who should live in stiff patience
under the stupor of contentment
and learn to live in want,
disgrace and anonymity.

Ornamentation and beautification
is for the well-off,
velvety gatherings to pamper
the puffed up ego.

Do you want to watch, feel and touch
softly round, white breasts;

to savour the rich, red wine
to lighten the heavy burden of living;
to enjoy fanciful poetry to inspire
the heart to new dizzy heights?

Pouring of pleasant words in ears
by some officious fools.
To show off and to assert vanity,
pride, hypocrisy and cruelty.

Power is everything;
fountain head of fame and glory
in the short human life history.
Otherwise what one is born for?

For the wretched ones
it has been the same forever;
to drag their drab existence
and beguile the time;
to face indignity, infidelity,
dishonor and humiliation.

To pass life in waiting
for things small and trivial,
right time and opportunities;
in helplessness and suffocation.

In ugliness, exploitation
and hunger, under the Oriental sky
There is no place for illusions,
life is lived as it is.

Whatever the period and place,
the have-nots are for suffering
and the haves are for enjoying.
Though in the long run
both are victims
of circumstances, and of time.

* * *

39. The Young Old Man

What should I look at,
the bulging belly, sagging cheeks,
all pleasures turning vapid.
The rising blood pressure,
backward going date of birth,
fast approaching day of death.

Or the fast fading dreams.
The vast golden sea shore,
the snow clad peaks of hills,
white breasts slyly winking,
fast approaching chilling knells.
Hide and seek of life and death.

The last rituals over a body
with no warmth, no wishes,
silent, with slightly open lips,
cold bones scattered sans ceremony,
only some last moments,
dying music, distorted by time.

* * *

40. To Be Rich

To be rich is something.
Yes, the people actually change,
acquaintances, relatives, friends—
all change.

They worship you like a God.
Otherwise you are a slave.
To be obeyed, like a demi-god
is something.

And, moreover, people agree
to your opinion, start believing
in you and the things
become available to you.

Sometimes, even the humans,
to be used or misused.
Either as a friend, relative
or a plaything.

Besides, it fulfills dreams;
dreams of a life time, only once.
Otherwise, what are dreams for,
if not materialized?

And that's the consummation.

If you depart satisfied;
well, what more do you want,
if your lust is satiated?

If all your passions are fulfilled,
if all enemies are vanquished.
What more do you aspire
in this limited life period?

* * *

41. What Else Is Life?

The middle-aged man danced,
with awkward steps and unsure gestures,
hopping on both legs, like a toad.
With some crisp currency notes
held in his flailing hands
to be scattered, and the children
jostling to pick them, like beggars,
their fathers sipping their whiskey.

What was he doing?
Why was he dancing,
with worn out body and heart?
Certainly not to woo a damsel
nor even to please his aging wife
or his friends or children.
But just to display his joy
for his nephew's wedding.

What else should he do?
After amassing a lot of wealth,
he was proving, to himself and others
that he was alive.
That he was on this side of the line.
Remembering faintly his father,
uncles, friends, who were dead.

What else was life or living
except to dance,
with your own people,
young and old, ugly and fair,
after a few pegs of whisky,
before a sumptuous dinner,
and before sleeping soundly.

Doing something before that eternal sleep!

* * *

42. The Company of Humans

Where there are people
there is evil.
So I thought of migrating
to a place in the hills
and live there in peace
like our great saints who
achieved salvation there,
sans men, women, old and young.

But there would be no company.
No friends or relatives
or foe, for that matter,
to love and hate.

No doubt, there will be
reptiles and mammals,
elephants, deer and lambs,
but also snakes and wolves.

How can they be friends?
Have you ever seen a snake
calling you by name,
raising its taut hood, saying,
"Hey, Stetson, how are you?"
or a lion roaring with laughter,
and then telling you
a joke about his beloved?

The idea abhorred me.
I rejected it completely.
Rather I decided to stay
and enjoy my human company.

* * *

43. Dead Past

The past dies in an instant,
though it is always alive in mind.

Yesterday I also was haunted
by my childhood days
and enjoyed lingering there,
in the remote memory lanes.

Layers and layers of illusion.
But howsoever pleasant,
it had ceased to exist.
It could not revive.
I can never be in the lap
of my boyhood, really
nor see the fresh world
through my innocent eyes.
Though most beautiful, it was dead.

Like the charming girl next door,
who was killed in an accident,
now lying dead on the floor.
Ravishingly beautiful,
plump cheeks, half exposed breasts,
the object of sensual desires;
to be possessed and loved.
But just till you touch her,
motionless, colorless and cold.

So you cannot enter into the past.
You can just look behind,
and see it like a mirage
from a long distance
and enjoy in it to that degree,
without touching it actually.

* * *

44. Unpleasant Situation

The human situation
is neither happy nor sad.
It is just unpleasant.
Blooming life is not offered
gracefully on a plate.
It has to be earned, won.

To rise, to stand,
to be healthy and rich
and to survive—
it requires ceaseless climbing,
sweat, pain, and risk,
which is unpleasant.

Self-control and self-denial
do not emit joy and pleasure.
Even when mother or brother calls
or the child makes demands.
What seems pleasant,
surely does not lead to full life.

Once in a while it is pleasant.
A warm day in a week,
a sunny hour in a long foggy day.
Or some years in a long life time
may be joyous and gay.
But mostly life is unpleasant.

45. What Next?

When I was a child
I desired for sweets
and hankered after toys,
craved for them;
rapturous when I could grab them,
sad and gloomy when denied.

When the child bloomed into youth
same thing happened.
Though the targets
were now different.
Supple, fair, youthful creatures
were the goals.
I literally dreamt about them,
day-dreamed of a particular one.

If they complied with my wishes
I was ecstatic;
and fretful and gloomy
when I was rejected;
rather harshly by one of them,
who looked a queen to me, then.

Though after some two score years,
one day I saw her in a busy street;
middle-aged and so commonplace.

Those rosy cheeks of her
wrinkled, pale and worn out
by time and worries of living.
An ordinary child with her,
accompanied by an old fool,
perhaps her husband,
did not seem to me the luckiest one.

Our eyes met.
And she averted the glance,
perhaps remembering me
and my disgusting advances,
as I was reminded
of her furious rebukes.
And realizing the futility of it all.
(dead, ugly past marring the present!)

Now I am also in my middle years.
I want to play
but with what money can buy
or power can extract,
as fruits yielded by the boughs
bent down forcibly.

I feel exalted
when the game is smooth
and my rival, vanquished
obeys me like a slave;
and resentful and sulky
when my attempts are thwarted.

I passed the first and
the second stage fairly well.

But wonder now
whether the present will pass off
like the early phases
or carried up to the grave.

After this what next?
I think in old age.
All these secular urges
will soon be forgotten
and worship of God
will be the next passion.

As old saints often profess
that all is vanity and futility.
Only His name is true and eternal
and will suit the purpose
of wading out smoothly
from this life, only one.

But my mother in her eighties,
instead of going to temple
for prayer and obeisance,
and chanting God's name in reverence,
is busy in humdrum routine.
Worries about money
and her supremacy
among her family members
and neighbours,
with all the rustic villagers.

She does not seem
to have crossed this middle muddle,
and perhaps will jump

to the other side
in a single stride.
Who knows what proves
right, proper and worthwhile
to sustain this long life.

* * *

46. Decline

Full to the brim
with overflowing joy and happiness
on this fair day of the fairest month
of my years when living longer
seems just getting older.
Cool breeze of departing March
caressing my last good years.

I don't want more.

Content with God's blessings,
saved from sudden catastrophes,
having achieved what I aspired for
(though there is no limit
even up to the last moment).

What is there but to wait
for the graceful departure?
Where to go after ascending
the highest precipice?

But to descend!

After soaring high like the proud eagle,
only to land down to the dusty earth.

* * *

47. Forward Movement

There is no moving back
from the present,
or the present turned future,
as when you are exactly
in the middle of a deep river,
breathless and exhausted,
the only course is to swim ahead.

You can dream about dreams,
but the past won't revive.
Neither can you wish it back
nor wrench it away
from your present time.

It sticks to you like this world,
forever, from beginning to end.
You are in it as it is in you.
Though it is easy to just go off
like a bullet in the outer space,
with no weight and no force,
still rushing into infinitude.

To survive without force!
To drag the existence,
nameless, friendless, aimless.
Living just like a worm,
or as a pig, mouthing garbage.

Move ahead, like the clear rivulet
through the silent hilly forests.
He who moves forward,
sooner or later achieves the goal.
The fight of the warrior will go on
unto the last breath that
utters the final adieu to the world.

* * *

48. Work and Life

My last romantic years
were slipping away speedily,
never to return again
(if there are no more lives).

And I was busy
frantically earning money,
revolving in drab,
mechanical routine work.

I was chasing the elusive dream
of money, riches unlimited.
All that to enjoy life
which is fleeting, anyway.

Is life meant for this drudgery?
To sweat and be yoked thus
to earn my bread
and not for joy and romance.

It is right, I thought,
that I am engaged so.
Physically and mentally;
morally and socially.

And so I am bound.
Otherwise I would let loose
my physique and spirits
and spoil myself.

* * *

49. Icarus

What was desired
and what is achieved!
Dream was the sky,
the fall was steep on the rock.

Why the grand flight
when the wings were fake?
Icarus was not ignorant
and still dared the adventure.

* * *

50. Man's Destiny

Sons and daughters going berserk,
the authority bent upon sucking
the last drop of energy and blood
out of the helpless, and
the neighbor inciting the neighbor
to poison peaceful living.

Poverty blocking the paltry
means of relief and dignity,
physique giving way to
strange incurable modern maladies.

What to control,
and how to control?

Is there any use of controlling man?
Or to let go everything
in the tornado of circumstances,
like the body projected in space
with no hurdle and resistance
except the ultimate fatal collision?

Or to walk blind
like the unearthly ghosts,
oblivious of earthly things,
to be deaf to the heart rending cries
and not to see the seen world.

51. Our Fate

What intense pain and anguish,
the burning sting of suffering
can befall human beings;
uncalled for, uninvited, undeserved
like a bolt from the blue!

The son gets out of control,
runs away from fatherly home,
the wife crosses the sanctity
of domestic hearth, to enjoy
the forbidden alien embraces.

A drunken father beats the family
who look to him for help, defense.
One is behind bars, killed
a friend enemy in a brawl.
And thus we humans suffer.

Life, considered to be elixir
turns out to be venom,
intolerable, fatal and bitter.

Some are overburdened with
the cursing ugly hag, poverty,
staggering through leaden life.

If luckily you wade through
half your years free of these,
the last nail which is stuck
is physical disease,
the cousin of old age.

Some rotten tissue never lets you
enjoy your meal, drink or breath
and leaves you only in the grave.

And last but not least,
the fear of death
before the death itself!

* * *

52. What to Do?

At the fag end of the journey,
when you could count
the approaching milestones,
the years, one by one,
you are baffled.
What to do, what not to do?

To grab the hidden treasure,
to wallow in the mire
of sensual orgies.
To squander health and wealth
in the final desperate bet
to regain all the pleasures.

To gather broken pieces of honour,
or to clutch the waning vitality,
repent and pray
and meditate in your prime
and earn the religious peace.
Prepare for the next phase.

Or stiff-necked, maintain status quo.
Mourn some more deaths
and celebrate a few weddings;
watch him rise to glory,

the arch rival fall to disgrace.
Monotonous flow of dull humanity.
To live normally,
and to depart silently,
even in the midst of the show.
To breathe in the stupor
of opium, of illusions, of romance,
like the silent oak tree.

On the fast slippery decline,
in such a hurry.
What to do, what not to do?
Or what to undo,
indelible addictions, responses,
or the past blunders and follies?

Sometimes it seems worthwhile
to drink the whole time
of the life which remains
at a single draught;
gulp down a mouthful
of sweetmeat of life at once.

Like the man about to drown,
gasping for breath
for the last grand sight
of the great blue sky,
the lush green lofty hills,
sinking, drowning, suffocating.

Whom to obey and what to believe!
Where are the wise men

who are the guides, the torch bearers?
But for them you grope in darkness;
though the choice is entirely yours.
One can't drift aimlessly for ever.

* * *

53. Marooned

When cruel life
like a nagging wife
leaves no recourse to you;
just marooned on an island
bounded by the salty sea
you are threatened by beasts.

Like a helpless frog,
prostrate on the dissection table
with limbs tightly pinned.
No help emanates from any side,
sympathy is not showered,
even when most desired.

No soft voice willing to console,
nothing inspires the mind
and the soul but itself.
Everything is within us
like in a seed, hidden, vital,
breathing, alive and powerful.

The soul, ultimate primeval source
of purity, serenity and peace.
Great is he
who can give and gives it.
He lives and grows
like a stolid tree, rooted firmly.

Rest is common humanity;
most of them drift merely
like icebergs in the vast sea
in search of solid ground,
or just dissolve away
in the heat of circumstances.

* * *

54. Who Should Sacrifice?

If I could sacrifice my pleasures,
my children will imbibe good habits,
will become good human beings
and will be happy.
If not, they would be like me,
uncontrollable, without self-restraint.

But how can that be?
My father gave full rein to his desires.
I saw him gulping greedily
from his Victorian china cup,
putting the country liquor bottle
safely in his lap.

So I followed his tradition.
Should I sacrifice my life, only one?
Or should I enjoy it, only one?
And let them go astray.
Who would sacrifice?
Theirs is more important than mine.

One generation will have to suffer,
to develop good character,
and only one can satiate in orgies
to perpetuate evil and ill culture.
That is how the traits are received
from one generation to the next.

55. People

People and people
here, there, everywhere.
Men, women, young and old
white, black, rich and poor.

In the bazaars, in the colonies
in towns, in villages
in buses, trains, carts and trams,
in the air, on board the ships.

Then I went to the hills.
There again I met people
with their love and passion,
their envy and their quarrels.

Good people, bad people,
cunning, shrewd and cruel,
helpful, innocent and simple,
cooperative and merciful.

Sometimes they are a burden,
a heavy weight on my tender psyche,
sometimes they torture me,
often they frighten me.

But still I can't live without

the familiar faces of humans.
I cannot imagine living
where there are no people.

* * *

56. Reining in the Beast in Me

"Mr. Raj is dead!"
The news struck me
like a bolt from the blue.
I could not believe it,
the young healthy cunning man,
who just talked to me that afternoon,
never to be seen again.

He was run over by a speeding truck.
"Oh, no, it can't be true",
I sadly thought;
but he was dead anyway.

After the initial shock
I felt a curious sensation of relief;
he was my main rival
for the Chairman's election.
Now there was no hindrance
in my moving to the top.
The only hurdle had disappeared.

But I crushed this
feeling of relief, blaming
the crude and cruel beast in me,
and mourned his death.

I was sorry for his family,
the young gentle lady,
and her tender children.

I had felt like an animal.
But I had the brain of a human
and obliterated that pervert
emotion of useless elation.

My human wisdom and sympathy
reined in that bestial instinct.
Actually, it could have been me
in that fatal car that fateful evening.

I prayed to God
for his family and soul.

* * *

57. Dilemma

"Set me free now,
my heart will not find peace.
I feel choked and suffocated,
you are inviting me to die.
I want to fly in the sky
on the wings of fancy,
to be satiated with melodies.
Kind nature, go on pouring
your bounties and benedictions
till I leave my prison."

"But you will be a slave
of unknown, untamed powers
once out of here.
The farther you run away
the heavier the burden grows.
Calm yourself and suffer,
for through suffering alone
you can escape the cycle."

"But I will be mad if I stay."

"And you will be dead
if you leave thus in your vanity.
It is better to live mad
than dying with sanity."

58. The Dancers

They sang melodiously
and danced slowly, gracefully,
tapping their feet in rhythmic unison
as if in a dream sequence.
With an innocent shy smile
went round, round, and round.

Everyone was at her best,
fair and not so fair.
Moist, supple, muscular bodies
swaying, bosoms heaving
sensuously, gestures of warmth,
bursting with passion underneath.

It happens with everyone.
I also sang and danced once.
It was so sweet and joyous.
I can sing now too, though
the white fleshy breasts
fail to stir the mad passion.

Life is really lived
ere it is lived the half way,
sweetest when it begins,
like your first trip to the hills,
unaware of its flow and movement,
ignorant of the journey's end.

59. The Dog Who Lost His Way

That dog trotted at a steady pace,
panting with his tongue dangling
sideways out of his open mouth,
tail unnaturally straight,
cautious eyes peering all around
for crouching enemies.

He had a rare poise, rhythm, grace;
had traveled a long distance,
but was not sure of his destination.
Fear was writ large on his face;
surely he had strayed from his area
and his master's secure house.

Now he was frightened, confused,
not certain where to go,
not clear how to reach there,
how to face the two-legged foe,
moreover, the aggressive brethren,
and where to settle down.

Just like man left on this earth!
But with undaunted, determined pace,
he kept on running tirelessly
to reach his destination.

* * *

60. The Gypsies

After having erected their
tenements, having arranged water,
fuel, setting crude implements;
after bribing the bully cop,
the gypsies finally settled down
and wove their baskets.

Amid the naked children playing,
the old were working,
like machines, callously,
smoking *biri* amid cheap utensils,
having suffered life, now waiting
for death patiently.

Two women were quarrelling,
abusing each other
in strange violent language,
flailing their hands wildly
(one even hit other with a dung cake).
All this for trivial things.

I wondered why they fought.
They had no common boundaries.
No farms, no poultry, no shops,
no territories like the German and French.
But were still jealous of each other,
each bent upon destroying the other.

This was all about human nature,
coexistence, social, human living.
Rivalry and enmity never die,
whether naked with a pointed
stone in hand, to hit the other,
or with weapons more civilized.

* * *

61. Growth in Society

Whether you are big and tall,
rich, mighty and influential;
gather name and fame,
or poor, weak and small.

You are so in a crowd,
community of humans,
not in the vacuum
of a desert or an island.

You grow in stature
in society of humans.
You are also stunted
to an ugly dwarf there.

* * *

62. Light and Darkness

The overwhelming darkness
is spreading menacingly in the north,
the surging black clouds
mixing together as in a conspiracy,
like evil.

But the rays of mighty sun
are beginning to pierce through
the dark green mango trees,
some fully, some partly covered,
with raw blossoms.

They are spreading
brightness in the east
through dense Ashoka trees
and the heavy gloom.

The surf white butterfly
set against the sky,
the snow white crane gracefully
flying against clouds murky.

But in the east the sunlight
undefeated by the threatening
shadows of despondency
proves the north wrong.

63. The Beginning of Day

And the great day began
in the city.
The vehicles thundered through
the choked streets.
The shopkeepers in the bazaar
began worshipping their deities.

Sprinkling water over
the sacred safes, scales and
devising dubious means to fleece.
The clerks groomed tidily,
sharpening their wits
to outwit their clients.

The boys all preparing
for the hectic schedule
of eve-teasing till late in the bazaar.
And the damsels, like Belinda,
arming themselves slyly
for the fit occasion.

It was not like the day of yore,
when it all began
with lowing of the cows
taken to the fields at dawn.
The oxen ready for their toil,
like their master, in the fields.

The house-wives plying
for the daily bread for all.
All hands and hearts for day's work,
everybody chanting contentedly
Ram-Ram, *Hare Ram*,
in different hymns.

The lust for money
was never absent.
But it was not so sharp,
painful, ruthless and blind.
It did not sting the aspirant
and the victim alike.

But it is always so.
Who knows this scrambling
seems sweet and golden
a few years hence,
contrasted with the future
years of fiery turbulence.

* * *

64. Mr. Birju? He Killed Himself

They told me Birju was dead;
killed himself on a railway track.
Deplorable, unfortunate,
and unimaginable fact.

Such a strong, healthy,
confident man of common sense,
who showed the path of hard reality
and proper conduct to the masses.

When we were children,
he appeared so authoritative, tall;
a formidable boss and chieftain
who had to be obeyed by all.

And he killed himself—
because he could not tolerate
the present, the modern age.
His own was already left behind.

His uncultured grandchildren
did not understand him
and could not look after him.
Above all, they refused to obey him.

So from a stern commander
he was reduced to a wretched beggar.
He could not live that life
and so died by choice.

Life is not gained by choice.

* * *

65. The Flowing Stream

Life does not flow
like a clear stream for
you to plunge in
and feel the coolness
in the sweltering heat.
It runs by its own logic
and necessity, for all,
the departed and the following.

They could not stop Ghalib,
or make Shakespeare tarry
to sing just one more song.
Alexander could have conquered
some more kingdoms.
Socrates might have rendered
the human race wiser
by another discourse.

No one could wait.
Nobody could be waited for.
The flux is so ruthless and fast.
How can I? A mere atom
of sand on the vast shore.
The kith and kin lament in vain.
Even the whole civilization
cannot defer the departure.

66. As Good as Dead

Slowly the man eclipses;
name, fame, identity
all fade away from the scene
and public memory.

No, not with his death,
even while he is breathing
people forget him.
His name, work, achievements—
all disappear.

Like the sun when though
it is still there in the west
with its power and glory lost,
its brightness waned
as good as set.
And you feel its absence.

So every man loses his.
When someone asks indifferently
"Is John still alive?"
And someone replies as casually
"No, he passed away last summer".

Many artists of colours,
clay, melody and words,

celebrities of yore,
are totally neglected and forgotten
by the ungrateful public
though still very much alive
in this same world.

The old leaders and generals,
who have fought many a war;
who have witnessed history,
nay, modified history
are forgotten in their last phase.

Just erased out of the memory
of their contemporaries.
Nor are they part
of memories of the youth.
The person loses his presence
before he actually dies.

* * *

67. Prayers and Pains

Somehow it seems
that all the prayers
rituals and donations
are for the relief
from pain and fear.

Fear of fight and war
the thundering dangers
diseases and disorders
known and unknown
seen and unseen
which is the lot
of all human beings.

All logical and orthodox
exercise is used to ameliorate
the terror and anguish
though they are more often
accomplished in the name
of religion charity,
salvation and philanthropy.
But still they come
and have to be borne.

* * *

68. I Couldn't Phone a Friend

That's how they knock you dead.
No chance, no time,
not a single opportunity
either to think or imagine
or to actually enter
the world of imagination,
the dizzy illusions
which could sustain you.

In the labyrinth of social customs
you can't even phone a friend,
not to speak of seeing one,
intimately, face to face.

It is really dreadful to live
in this ancient civilization.
With unsheathed swords
two dark naked musclemen
standing erect, ominously,
prying into your privacy.

Ever the tribes of humans
are guarding you.
Is it only for the collective
code of the establishment?
No life beyond this,
and one granted only once.

I remember the days
when the newly-wed couple
couldn't find a place
to sleep together.
I am far better placed
and enjoy so many freedoms.

* * *

69. The Control Freak

There comes a time in life
when things go out of control.
(They had never been in control, though.
But the very illusion
that everything is under control
sustains and smoothes living.)

The rulers do not rule properly;
youths are rude,
friends and relatives
do not act as you wish.
Neighbors pass nonchalantly,
ignoring you totally.

Parents' demands appear unjustified.
Sons and daughters
turn wayward;
what to say of wife.

Even your physique disobeys you;
strange malfunctions are
detected in the system,
which even defy medication.

Life is reduced merely
to passing days,
and is measured against
the ticking of the clock.

70. The Crying Infant

The little child cried incessantly.
And all efforts to pacify him failed.
He cried despite the efforts
of his mother, father
and other relatives, male and female;
he cried and cried frantically.

The passengers in the bus were moved.
Some said he was hungry
other attributed it
to the humid heat of July.

The third perhaps was right;
he said, "He is scared of the
absurdly dressed *sadhu*
standing near him.

He was frightened and weeping.
But who can escape weeping,
loud or silent, in this world;
the pains and worries of life?

The infant was crying.
But he will have to weep
in youth also,
and in old age too.

He will always feel
anxiety and fear in this world.

The fear of boss and wife;
of separation from dear relatives;
of the enemy at home
and beyond the borders.

Horror of penury and diseases
will be his lot;
and so will be the dread of death;
and, no doubt, of the next birth.
He will have to pay
the price of life on this planet.

* * *